SELLING RIGHT
IN THE WORLD
OF RETAIL

SELLING RIGHT IN THE WORLD OF RETAIL

INCREASING YOUR
PERCENTAGES IN CLOSING
THE SALES IS AN ONGOING,
PRACTICAL ART

OYERONKE A. (DUROJAIYE) LAWOYIN

LIBRARY OF CONGRESS CONTROL NUMBER:		2007909257
ISBN:	HARDCOVER	978-1-4257-4650-6
	SOFTCOVER	978-1-4257-4649-0
	EBOOK	978-1-4628-1427-5

Rev. date: 05/03/2021

To order additional copies of this book, contact:
Xlibris
844-714-8691
www.Xlibris.com
Orders@Xlibris.com
575618

CONTENTS

To the Glory of God and in gratitude
to my employers, colleagues, and numerous customers
having provided me the opportunity to do this work.

Foreword

Ultimately, the only two attributes that any of us bring to our jobs are our attitudes and preparation. We all have varying skill levels, educational backgrounds, and God-given talents. Some of you are highly intelligent, and some of us are like a pastor who once said, "I'm not the brightest person I know." And it doesn't matter.

If you've been in the working world for a while, you've probably had the opportunity to work with some gifted individuals, some highly unmotivated, and the majority of persons in the morass. So why do some people excel while others, even the gifted, sometimes do not?

Selling Right in the World of Retail is a compendium of stories of some of the most successful retail men and women and entrepreneurs. The reader gets a brief look at their "rise to the top." As varied as their stories, their commonality was that they all were proactive, positive, and prepared. The second half of this work outlines practical applications for the employee as well as the employer.

Oyeronke Alake Lawoyin or Ronke came to the world of U.S. retail business after being a public administrator in a developing African economy. Her approach to retail selling has been that it is an opportunity to serve. And in serving, she has learned, excelled, and now conveys her observations. Much of the book is geared to prepare the employee, but the underlying observations are geared to enhance employer strategy and execution in a more competitive retail environment.

John M. Windelberg
President,
TRIGEMS INC.

Acknowledgments

I have been blessed by the quality of help from different sources.

My husband, John Oladapo Lawoyin, has shown understanding and given support. He read the manuscript and offered a wealth of prized suggestions. My children have always believed in me and have been a source of encouragement on each step of the way. I thank my grandchildren, being very much around me without causing more of a distraction than they did.

My late parents, Moses Abiola and Florence Adedoyin Durojaiye, earlier in my life, introduced me to retail merchandising. Late Mrs. Susannah Lawoyin shared her personal experience in snacks retail merchandising with me.

Late Mrs. Mary Olateju Ogunniyi, who introduced me to a larger scale of retail merchandising, was a great mentor of mine. She mentored me while I ran a retail business of my own. I have not given up yet.

Robin Cahan was kind enough to read my manuscript and challenge me to do other writings. Ben, more of my son than a son-in-law, has been my in house as computer mentor and diligently helped me overcome my early challenges on the computer.

Ms Susan Mowen, Ms Mary Diane Wickham, Ms Charlene Macalus, Professor Ruth Okediji, and Tomas Felcan, who out of their very busy schedules were able to read and advise on my work, I appreciate your determination and love to support me.

I am very grateful to John Windelberg, who out of his very busy schedule was able to write my foreword.

My profound gratitude goes to my numerous customers who made each working day a new opportunity to do what I have always loved doing—customer service!

Last, but certainly not the least, I appreciate the efforts of my publisher, Xlibris, for their final efforts on this work—dotting my i's and crossing my t's

Introduction

This book spurs from almost nine years of retail experience in the American economic system. It is my joy, regret, many times unrewarding but worthwhile pursuits. These situational moods provide an underlying impetus to write this book.

My objective in writing this book is multipurpose. Several times, I have pondered on why anyone would want to read it. After all, there are thousands of good business books out there to pick from. Further pondering led me to the realization that no knowledge subject is exhaustive. There is always something to add.

The impetus to write this book was sparked off in 2003 when I became the winner of a contest on "Reduction of Shrinkage" in the store where I worked. It was a short but heart-moving ceremony wherein I was given a monetary award. I also regularly won top scores for credit card application referrals. The desire to share my experiences moved me to write.

After many years of teaching and working as a public administrator in a developing economy, I relocated to a developed economic society and found myself taking up a job as a customer service associate at a department store. I had earlier on in life been taught retail by my mother and elder sister. I had also managed a retail business of my own. My plan was to work for a job in my field of specialization. My academic preparation as a social scientist and my love for people worked together to stabilize my emotional attachment to the new job. That realization kept me focused. Rather than be overcome by the feeling of rejection, I took up the challenge, and I decided to make it profitable.

I want to focus on retail organizations for their nature of large staff turnover according to my observation. I believe that a book such as this will encourage their staff to stay on and make their places of work better places than they have found them. When a new associate is being appointed, this book could be a source of information on what he needs to know about his new job, so he can give his best. This is no claim that everyone who reads the book will stay on at the job, but that most people will find the information that will make them feel more comfortable working retail. The staff may not be hopping from one retail organization to another because they have little or no knowledge of the retail world.

This book is expected to bridge the gap between information sources from a library and information from the companies' manuals, which are needed for sales professionals to improve their customer service skills so they can continue to grow and make a profit. I am hopeful that companies will be interested in purchasing the book and that they will place it in the workers' break rooms or libraries where sales associates may be given the opportunity to check it out at their convenience. I know that most sales professionals are at work late and may not be able to go to a public library as much as needed or find the time to read on the Internet. Companies and retail organizations and individuals can use this as a handbook for training their staff. I have tried to draw resources from library books, which can inform salespeople about what help people have to offer them in their sales.

There are misconceptions held by so many people about retail, which is a great profession with many opportunities to help people. Retail is business about people. The associate can help people to find good products that may not be known to them. You could lead them to love what they did not like at first sight. You can encourage them to see needs they can take care of immediately and should not wait till later. You can make them do more than they thought they could. An associate can make a difference in people's lives by his or her action. He or she can make a difference in the employer's business. The associate can be effective in the performance of his or her job.

Shoppers and customers are involved in retail business as well. This is focused on customers who may be interested in appreciating how the retail business operates in their interest and how they can be part of the solution to the existing problems of retail. Besides, as customers try to be their best, they will receive the best.

The information in this book may be useful to all levels of businesses whether wholesale, retail, or a combination of both. Retail may be considered an offshoot of wholesale, and both levels of business operations require a basic functional knowledge of each other.

Beyond the borders, businesses in developing countries and elsewhere could benefit from the information in the book since these are societies where there is a shortage of books. Retail businesses spring up rapidly, and the goal of business in these countries as in others is to make money. There is much to know about the propriety of maximizing profit and opportunities for wealth.

In the opening chapter, I will be reviewing some ideas from the works of different writers on salesmanship. Their books are very useful and could be read in depth if the people I address in this work can go to the library to drink deep. It is worth the while for a person going into retail to have a reasonably adequate prior knowledge of the requirements of the trade. If for instance, a rather impatient or unfriendly person is contemplating retail work and he comes into contact with this book, a glimpse of it may be a help for self-evaluation.

In this valuable book, I wish to inform my readers of the substance of what the book writers under reference envision the salespeople could be and what their establishments should do to help them.

For retail customers who may be interested in navigating the world where they constantly find themselves, the book may come as a help. The education this book offers them may make it unnecessary for them to ask the usual questions that busy associates are usually asked.

It is amazing to know how much of the human nature and character could be observed in the sales procedure and in the interaction between the customers and the associates. There are different displays of moods, behaviors, expressions, words, and acts. Some customers may be considerate of the store management and staff whereas others may not care whether or not the store is hurt by their behavior. A customer may buy a pair of shoes and wear them until they are old. This pair may later be brought back to the store with flimsy excuses, and the customer may insist on an exchange with new shoes or refund in money. Anything short of these will become unacceptable to him. Another customer may not insist on replacement and may seek advice about what style of shoe or size or color may be more suitable. He may be prepared to pay a new price.

A customer may be the first to greet the associate no matter how prepared the latter is to welcome him. Another customer may fail to respond to the greeting of the associate. Some customers will heartily chat with the associate whereas others will keep sealed lips during the transactions. At the end of the transaction, some customers may not respond to "thank you."

Good customer service is the key to successful business, and an associate is expected to keep his cool in spite of what the character or behavior of the customer would be. Patience then becomes a vital attribute in retail. The larger the organization, the greater is the need for patience.

It is also my purpose to encourage people to go into retail jobs. The social as well as spiritual satisfaction of doing a good job in retail is enormous. The retail world provides job fulfillment for people who choose to work as professionals. Regardless of their religious sect, there is a good opportunity for affecting lives through the care and love expressed by the associates to the customers.

At the point of service, the associate could be constantly informed. Shoppers will talk about the weather while they are being served. Visitors who are in the country on vacation or training courses or are just visiting also come to the malls. They have interesting information to share with the associates while they are in the line and are being served.

I personally feel comfortable in the world of retail and would want people who read this book to learn. This work is on retail operation. My purpose is to lead people to identify with and embrace the retail job as a profession. I want to make available a book that is easy to read, that will inform readers in general about available literature on businesses including retail information.

I believe the world economy could experience a revolution if the employers and employees in businesses could generally understand how vital it is to have a book on retail.

Chapter 1

Review of Books Dealing with Sales

When I was looking for sources of relevant information on retail, I ran into books that have been published on how to be successful businesspeople. Since I was greatly impressed by what they had to say about sales, I would like to relate my understanding of their messages to you along with my own personal comments in some cases.

There are many books out there that address retail issues in various ways and are relevant to the job of retail. I have been able to focus in this book some of the views of writers from these books and, therefore, attempted to wet the appetite and encourage the reader to take the advantage of a reference library even in their work break room or work library.

Wrong Concepts of Selling

One of the authors whose work I read is William T. Brooks, writer of *Niche Selling: How to Find Your Customer in a Crowded Market.*

An identified wrong concept of selling is to apply desperate pressure to get a customer to patronize a business. Brooks (1992, ix) found that salesmen who adopt this style "emphasize their comparative selling price and deliver scripted sales representations."

Brooks also identified as wrong the hiring of people who wear clothes as if their personality is the commodity on sale, but who do not back their appearance with reliable service. The author said that the sales forces do not understand the role of their marketing department and cannot work in harmony with what is not familiar to them. The sales method, according to Brooks, is unacceptable because the salespeople focus on what the company wants from the sales relationship and not what the prospects want. He observed that people who are so treated feel confused and uncomfortable and rarely make buying decisions. Brooks (1992, 5) cited the Pareto principle known as the "80/20 Rule," which becomes the practice when only "20% is on customer focus, 80% is on self and product"

Brooks also identified outdated approaches of sales training and said there are misconceptions in sales training philosophies, which emphasize that to succeed one only learns the features of the company's products or services.

The author said that products are not weapons with which to move customers to "surrender" their money (1992, 13).

Markita Andrews, author of *How to Sell More Cookies, Condos, Cadillacs, Computers . . . and Everything Else*, advised that salespeople should resist thinking about everything that could go wrong in selling. She said they are not to stick only to a certain strategy and think "selling is fun" (1986, 56). Andrews said people are not born with the art of selling, but that the skills are to be learned so that customers would not be bored with explanations of products.

In *Smart Guide to Starting a Small Business,* Lisa Rogak identified that the wrong concept of selling starts right from the advertising stage when entrepreneurs focus on their business rather than on their customers.

Michael LeBoeuf, author of *The Perfect Business: How to Make a Million from Home*, said there is a problem when a businessman fails to recognize the difference between what he wants and what the customer wants and needs.

LeBoeuf (1996, 85) observed that most businesspeople emphasize what they want and further observed that most people are interested in closing the sale and have no effective plan on hand to continue where the sale ends. The author advocated that the closing of a sale is to be used as a stepping stone to the beginning of a new relationship with the customer and prospect.

In *Mastering Your Way to the Top, Secrets for Success*, Joe Girard identified the importance of commitment to people especially the customers and prospects. Girard (1995) expressed that some businesses do not commit enough time and planning to their business relationships.

Robert L. Jolles, author of *Customer Centered Selling*, pointed at faulty sales training as a reflection of the wrong concepts of sales. According to Jolles, most sales businesses prepare their employees to articulately dump features and solutions on their customers. Most salespeople are considered knowledgeable about their products, but they lack the skills to sell them.

Jolles (1998) said that some salespeople become confrontational with their customers once an objection is raised by the customer because they have not received a proper training.

In *The Heart of the Sale: Making the Customer's Need to Buy the Key to Successful Selling, Garry Mitchell (1991, 3) identified the following wrong concepts of selling:*

1. Concentration on the product
2. Use of wrong probes and too many closed ended questions
3. Giving of faulty sales training

Mitchell found that salespeople needed not try to sell to someone who does not have the need of their products because they will make no sales if prospects do not want what the salesperson wants to offer. According to Mitchell, (1995,5) people will buy what they want to buy, and it is the responsibility of the industry to plan an approach to selling, which will "make sales efforts coincide with the needs of the buyer and take advantage of the customer's interest and readiness to buy." Mitchell further said that most sales training and sales literature are focused on the salesperson's activity in "selling" and not on the part of the buyer's reactions. This is considered a serious lapse when it is realized that sale depends more on a set of reactions on the part of the buyer than it does on the actions of the seller. No matter how good a salesperson or his techniques can be, he cannot force a sale on an unwilling buyer. (1991)

Mitchell agreed with the observation of the other authors that sales training is inadequate. He saw aggressiveness as a negative action since it creates resistance and results in loss of sales. He conceptualized assertiveness as good selling art. As Bob Kimball, (1994) writer of Successful Selling, established "salesmanship" is not a talent, and it is wrong to see salespersons as people to be avoided. Kimball said that people do not buy "products" and "features," they buy benefits. He agreed that people hate to be sold and that professional salespeople are not to sell anyone. Like Mitchell, Kimball believed in "assertiveness of the sales person in assessing the customer's buying style and sensitivity and in getting the sale by helping them to buy the way they like to buy" (1994, 21). Kimball identified inadequate training for salespeople. He recognized lack of good questioning skills in salespeople and saw that it could militate against closing a sale and taking advantage of after-close sales.

Right Concepts of Selling:

William T. Brooks explained in *Niche Selling* that it is not profitable for industries to go by the old concepts and methods of training for these reasons: (1) Customers have various other sources of buying the same or similar products that a particular industry or company may want to offer them; (2) Apart from the competing organizations, there are other available sources that can usurp the sales effort of an organization. These sources include the computer, industrial intelligence reports which are readily available and can duplicate a successful product or service (Brooks, 1992, ix). Brooks considered it expedient that industries diligently serve the long-term needs of their customers so that they can count on them with their trust. Brooks recommended that sales organizations determine what their buyers value most and point out the unique advantages of their product or service that address the customers' values. Brooks (1992) said that the focus is to be on the customers, and even in hard economic times the focus should never be taken away. Brooks saw the need for necessary support efforts from the sales force, marketing department, and the entire industry to focus on the same target—customer. Brooks said, "The Greatest Secret in Selling is showing people what they want most. Thereafter they will move heaven and earth to get it." (1992, 47) The salesperson working as a team with the entire organization should view himself as a needs-fulfiller for every prospect and customer. With this kind of focus, it becomes achievable for the salesperson to put emphasis on helping people to make a decision to buy and not on selling. Established in this work frame, the salesperson is more likely viewed as a welcome aide than one who will trigger negative emotions (1992, 64). To train salespeople to be efficient, Brooks said that their organizations are to appropriately implement and maintain specific techniques that will go beyond the needs of the organizations and be entirely on the needs of each customer. The salespeople who receive this kind of training are more likely to sell to the buyers' needs rather than sell a product or service.

Markita Andrews, author of *How to Sell More Cookies, Condos, Cadillacs, Computers . . . and Everything Else*, said that it is a right concept to sell what you like yourself, what you enjoy doing, and what people will need. Her opinion is that selling be done where people will need the products. She said that salespeople should sell themselves everywhere they go and not just their products because selling to her is part of the whole world. Andrews (1986) also said that selling is to be made interesting. According to her, selling is not just talking about the product, but about other things so that you get to know the customers, their needs, and on how to fulfill them. Andrews advocated making and keeping short- and long-term goals, which can be adjusted upward or downward according to circumstances.

Lisa Rogak, author of *Smart Guide to Starting a Small Business*, addressed the right concepts in selling your own business. She believed a salesperson is to be educated and given a great head start in the business. There is a need for the salesperson to get a good basic understanding of people and be taught the basic people skills that are needed in good communication with the customers. Rogak (1999, 137) addressed two marketing strategies and clearly stated that these will "convey positive messages to customers and thereby influence their buying decisions."

Michael LeBoeuf said that the right concept of selling is that a salesperson should create a perceived value so that customers can buy "benefits." He believed customers exchange money for something they believe will satisfy them more than the money they have to pay for it. What money does is the value and not money itself. People exchange their money for benefits and solve their problems. The salesperson is to be trained to solve the customers' problem by making them feel good about the service he gives to them. What he does, how well he does it, and how difficult it would be to replace him will determine how much money the industry can make. Salespersons are to be trained as effective communicators who are able to positively get people to do what they want. LeBoeuf (1996, 73) cites the examples of large successful companies like Corning and Motorola that believe in the concept of effective training as a means of successful business and require that all the employees spend a minimum of 5 percent of their time on the job training and learning new skills. It is reported that Motorola generates thirty dollars in productivity for every dollar spent on training within three years.

Like Andrews, LeBoeuf recommended that a salesperson believes deeply in what he sells and be eager to help as many people as possible by creating value on sharing the benefits of his products with them. LeBoeuf emphasized the need for positive communication on the part of the salesperson so that he can tailor his products and services to his audience, speak to them in their language, and get their attention and get them to buy his production and service.

In the book *Mastering Your Way to the Top*, Joe Girard describes "selling" as a "people business" and thereby advises that industries and salespeople, whatever their product or service, to recognize this as such and learn from their customers what they expect and demand. Girard (1995, 64) believes that businesses should build loyalty and win the confidence of their customers so that they can continue to sell. He admonishes the businesspeople to put in place steps and strategies to win their customers and overcome the obstacles that may be in their way of success. To stay on top of their businesses, the author recommends that they constantly and steadfastly create values for their customers.

Robert L. Jolles, author of *Customer Centered Selling*, in presenting his view of the right concept of selling, gave reasons why we need good salespeople. One reason is that there can be devastating consequences when people are left on their own to discover what they really need and the urgency with which they need it. It is this understanding of the nature of man that led Jolles to conclude that "people need a push once in a while to make a decision and that is why the focus should be on the customer and what could be done to help him decide to buy the products." (1995, 7) To Jolles, learning the art of selling is what no organization must compromise or rush. He said that the actual art of selling has little to do with specific features or products, but it has more to do with the art of persuasion. Since problems shape people's needs, Jolles thought the bigger the problem, the bigger the need and the more customers will pay for the solution whether it is for a service or a product. He further expressed that a salesperson is to be fully aware of this procedure of decision making on the side of the customers and learn to persuade them to fix whatever problems they may have at hand. Jolles says that linking customer needs to the benefits of the company's products will guarantee sales continuously. *Selling* by Jolles's definition is "taking an idea in your customers' minds and making them feel that they thought of it." (1998, 104) In expatiating on this concept, Jolles said that customers buy benefits that are the specific values, and the salesperson is to take advantage of the customer's search for benefits and link his solution (sale of his products or service) directly to the customer's needs. The author said that salespersons not only help the customers to understand their requirements, but also specify those requirements and earn the trust of the customer. Jolles said that the salesperson can seal up this trust relationship and be able to close a sale when he does not manipulate but persuade and clearly tie his solution to the customer's needs. Jolles (1998, 341) further stressed that "professional selling" is not about a couple of good ideas, but that it requires a "repeatable and predictable process" He was optimistic that there would be successful selling when the regular use of the right practice of the sale process becomes an unconscious act and develops competency in the salesperson. Accordingly, Jolles said that customer-centered selling is not a slogan, but it is a way of life; and he encouraged salespeople to accept this fact and practice it passionately (1998).

Garry Mitchell's approach to selling as expressed in his book *The Heart of the Sale* is that industries are to plan their sales efforts with the recognition of the customer's interests and wants and focus on those objectives because sale depends more on the buyers' reactions than on the actions of the salespersons.

Mitchell (1991) said that a good salesperson cannot possibly force a sale on an unwilling buyer by simply employing "good" sales techniques. He said that a salesperson should be trained to develop good negotiation tactics such as basic effective communication skills that can lead customers to make a positive decision to buy the product or service. He advised businesses to create advertisements that will coincide with the buyers' interests and values.

Bob Kimball, author of *Successful Selling*, saw "selling" as a "learned skill." He said, "Commensurate skills get people far, not techniques." (1975, 3)

Kimball argued that people buy for their reasons, which are based on the benefits to be derived from the product or service, and they do not buy because a salesperson can goad them to buy. He said that customers will buy from salespeople whom they like and trust and that trust is built on salespeople who focus on their customers, their needs, and their interests. Kimball (1975, 117) suggests that a salesperson should initiate a good rapport with the prospect, build the foundation of a business relationship by getting undivided attention of the prospect, talk less, and listen more. He saw this procedure of communication as what can lead the prospect to "discover the benefits of the products or service and buy."

Kimball further said that knowledge is the foundation power in selling, and industries are to give effective training to their staff who will handle the sales procedure so that customers and prospects can be helped to come to a decision to buy their products and services and continue to find value in them. According to Kimball, the salesperson is to "create power within him and learn more about the customer needs, buying motives and hot button." (1975, 123)

How Can the Right Concepts of Selling Be Put to Work?

William T. Brooks said that one approach to putting the right concept of selling to work is to understand the concept of change and take advantage of the opportunities of change to analyze, anticipate, and adapt to the changes. Brooks submitted that with the need for continuous adjustment and adaptation comes the need for acquisition of necessary knowledge such as knowledge of customers and how they arrive at their decision making, knowledge of people and their behavior patterns, and how to use this knowledge to stay on top of their businesses. (1992)

Brooks said further that the salespeople are to know themselves too and discover their relevant skills to selling. This knowledge, he added, will help the salesperson to be confident as he "possesses the accurate market knowledge and consistently applies the right skills." (1992, 23)

According to Brooks, (1992, 9) businesses are not to be "inner directed" on themselves, products, or companies, but be "outer directed" focusing on the deepest needs of customers and finding ways to fulfill those needs even in hard economic times. Customer's focus is adjudged by Brooks to be the only certain formula for success in selling because the industries and salespeople have the greatest impact on the customers when they focus on their needs.

In order to achieve the level of success, thus far said, Brooks expressed that there has to be a new direction in sales training. Learning the features of the company's products or services, vital as it is to training, can no longer be considered the whole picture. Brooks recommended an all-out effort on sales staff that is to leverage all resources (time, strength, skills, and structures) available in support of identifying and fulfilling customer needs. He recommended that the entire company force including salespeople and marketing staff are to align themselves to establish value structures that will enable them to become committed to customer-centered selling. Furthermore, Brooks said that the emphasis of salespeople should be on "helping people to make a decision to buy, and never on selling." (1992, 47)

Markita Andrews, author of *How to Sell More Cookies, Condos, Cadillacs, Computrers . . . and Everything Else*, says that a salesperson should use the five senses when he sells. She suggested that the first thing a salesperson has to sell is his person. Since he is the first step in selling, he has to sell himself before his products. This realization is to expose him to the knowledge of his skills, his emotion, and his understanding of the job he is doing. Andrews said that the knowledge of the businesses and his customer is "to help the sales person fit everything into his life." (1986, 1) The author stated that the salesperson is to be determined and be able to think ahead of time the things that could go right or wrong and on how to react to them effectively.

Setting short- and long-term goals and how to meet the goals at any specific period and the ability to make adjustments are actions recommended by Andrews. The author said that a salesperson could make his job interesting if he does not talk about "selling" all the time. She confirmed the importance of knowledge of the customer to successful selling when she said that "knowing everybody" is good for sales and "when the buyer ends up buying something she did not expect to buy, that's the work of a salesperson." (1986, 26)

Andrews recommended the tool of "listening harder than usual" for use in dealing with customers. She conveyed the message that salespeople are to be honest, polite, cheerful, neat, and have good manners and common courtesy in order to appeal to the customers. Andrews found that if these attributes are easily observable, customers will discover the salesperson and his products. (1986)

In Andrews's view, "The salesperson is to get the customers one by one and build up business, keep each customer, and regard him as important." (1986, 50) Furthermore, Andrew considered risk taking as an essential part of successful selling. "Risk," in the author's explanation, included "rejection" that should be skillfully handled by thinking through ahead of it and learning to live with it. She encouraged salespeople to do the things they dread so that it will make them less scary and not be afraid to make mistakes, get more involved in the selling business, and let their success with one customer lead to other customers.

In her book *Smart Guide to Starting a Small Business*, Lisa Rogak agreed with other authors that industries give their salespeople the equipment of knowledge through training. (1999) Salespeople in this way are to get good basic people skills needed for communication with customers. Rogak expressed the importance of politeness and treatment of every person that the salesperson meets in the course of doing business with the same kind of attention and respect that he expects from other people. Rogak further suggested that industries should know their direct competitors outside of their circle of customers so that they can get information that will help them to focus on value-driven services to their direct customers.

According to Rogak, business success can be enhanced by repeat customers whom he considers to be "the lifeblood" of any business. She also said that getting a repeat customer to come back is usually less expensive than getting a new customer to try out a business in the first place since most people need to receive several exposures to a company's message before they decide to check it out.

She also suggested that businesses and their salespeople should stress how their service or products can save a customer's time. She emphasized the need for consistency, which businesses are to ensure by sending the same message in all their marketing materials. Rogak's view was that businesses should distinguish themselves from competition by "focusing on developing a market message that sets itself apart from the competition and by offering products or services that will make them want to buy from them and not others." (1999, 140)

Michael LeBoeuf said that making a mission statement is a vital step to take to be a success in business. In his book *The Perfect Business*, he emphasized that it should be made known in a mission statement why a particular business exists—this should be the focus. He further said that there needs to be focus on time and energy to create values to be provided to the customers.

LeBoeuf was in consonance with the other authors on the importance of teaching the latest tools and techniques and communications with impact "so they can be clear and persuasive when dealing with the customers." (1996, 69)

In the effort to make a sale, LeBoeuf said that the salesperson is to handle an objection before the customer raises it. He advised the salespeople to listen and empathize with the customer and eliminate the objection. He found that the responsiveness may make the customer glad to hear from the salesperson, and that may elicit trust in the salesperson.

LeBoeuf recommended that salespeople are to employ their imagination to think up new products and services, find faster, cheaper, and better ways to get things done, and, thereby, make obsolete any type of competition. (1996)

In order to make his right concept of selling workable, Joe Girard, author of *Mastering Your Way to the Top: Secrets for Success*, recommended that salespeople are to see a picture of them successful and winning and not quitting. He said to get there and stay successful, the salespeople are "to acquire knowledge skills, the ability to set reasonable goals, sound judgment, determination, and continuous self-development." (1996, 7) The author further said that it is important to set clearly defined, flexible minor and major realistic goals so that they can be adapted to change as necessary. Girard suggested that industries are to train their staff to be goal and risk-taking oriented, knowledgeable, confident, and loyal. The confidence and loyalty thus built will win for the business the confidence and mutual allegiance with the customers so that they will buy at all seasons. Girard also found his law of 250: *The way you interact with people, the way you treat them, will be multiplied 250 times*, which is relevant to the success in business. (1996, 154)

Robert L. Jolles offered the concept of working from the interest of the customer so that success in business could be achieved. Nothing else seemed to matter to Jolles if you do not first center your selling processes on the customer. In his book *Customer Centered Selling*, he said that businesses are to first study the decision-making process, which is in three stages. In the first stage, the customer decides whether he wants to fix the problem or not. In the second stage, he asks himself what he needs to fix the problem bothering him, and at the last stage, he decides whom he will allow to fix the problem bothering him. Jolles said that if the salesperson "skillfully uses the questioning method repeatedly and predictably the process will lead to a customer's decision to buy and follow up on buying." (1998, 312)

He said that training is of vital importance in getting the salesperson to achieve the customer-centered selling aim of a business, and salespeople are to be taught that the whole basis of customer-centered selling revolves around customers' needs. He added that customers base their decision making on the benefits they derive from the company's products, and the salesperson needs to identify the specific value of the product to the customer and assist him in solving his problem. (Jolles, 1998)

The salesperson is to be trained in the questioning techniques, as this is critical to the opening up of advantages for the customer to talk to the salesperson.

Jolles said that the use of open-ended questions such as *what*, *where*, *when*, and *why* can help the customer who is otherwise reserved to get to talk and to expatiate on his questions and answers. He explained that the "closed" questioning technique provides the customer the opportunity to give a yes or no response, but does not give the customer an opportunity to expand on his answer. According to Jolles, the "closed" questions are introduced by *do*, *so*, *is*, *are*, *if*, *can*, *will*, and *would*; and they have benefits that they can be used to "control the conversation of a talkative customer, clarify an otherwise vague customer information, test and confirm information." (1998, 96) Jolles advised the salesperson to balance the use of the two types of questions and not overuse them in the sales cycle. An example of the error to watch is "What type of work do you perform? I mean, do you prepare client briefs?" (1998, 98)

Garry Mitchell, author of *The Heart of the Sale,* said that businesses are to plan their sales efforts to coincide with the wants of the customers and take advantage of their interests and readiness to buy. The author recommended the use of direct marketing, which is directed at those prospects that have most likely reached the buying stage and will buy immediately. Mitchell suggested, "Prospects and customers should be approached as people the salesperson wants to get to do something and not as people to sell something." (1991, 62) He further said that every objective of the seller has to be customer centered, and the seller is to have the right recipe for the buyer.

Bob Kimball, author of *Successful Selling*, said that salesmanship is "knowledge of the product or service, and knowledge of the customers and their needs; the competitors and the industry." (1994, 3) Kimball found that the skills needed to achieve the objectives of salesmanship are to be learned; and if people will put themselves in the customers' shoes, they will be able to take the focus off themselves and place it on the customers; and they will find people who will buy for their own reasons and not for the salespeople's. He emphasized that the salesperson is to help the customer get the benefits of his product or service. Kimball suggested that the salesperson is to be aware of himself, be all he can be, self-disciplined, achievement oriented, and honest. The salesperson, according to Kimball, needs to set goals and priorities in his planning. Also of importance is effective communication in selling. To Kimball, listening to the prospects and customers is an aspect of effective communication. He advised salespersons not to do more socializing than is necessary so that the customers do not see the salespeople as wasting their time. Rather than engage in unnecessary chitchat, Kimball said that the salesperson is to be alert and seek areas of common ground with the prospect to build a relationship that will extend beyond the current sale. He further recommended that the way a salesperson can sell more is to move into the product presentation and get the prospect and customer to talk by using questions judiciously and by listening to the customer.

Knowing the relative strengths and weaknesses of the competition can be an asset to the salesperson as this knowledge can help to focus on the unique selling points to emphasize in the presentation of the benefits of the product and service. Kimball considered "knowledge" as the foundation of power in selling because without it, the salesperson is nowhere and cannot get anywhere, but with it, the sky is the limit. (1994)

The salesperson's personality and attitude, Kimball said, can enhance the chances of getting the prospect and customer to buy more. Salespeople are encouraged by Kimball to be courteous, ethical, and decent so as to give a chance for people to like, respect, and do business with them. (1994)

Chapter 2

Networking in Retail

Interrelatedness of All Departments in the Retail Business

Most salespeople get employed and they go straight to the sales floor without being aware that there are other departments besides sales. These departments perform functions that are directly related to the sales department.

The salesperson needs to know them all so as to be able to function effectively. He is to be aware of how the activities of these different sections affect him and how he affects them.

The activities that go into the retail business make up the network system as follows:

The Visual Department

The visual department is an integral part of selling. Organizations and presentation of the merchandise at the department is a combined effort of the visual staff, the departmental managers, supervisors, and associates.

The colorizing, sizing, and sectional arranging of products are usually assessed by customers, and these will, to a large extent, determine what passion they will have in favor or against a business organization. Store organization is an on-going business of rearranging and transferring of products or merchandise sale after sale and day after day.

There will be products and events promotions and introduction of new products. The ultimate goal is to attract customers and make profit.

How to Present Merchandise/Products:

Some stores may have specialized services and may have the schedule of merchandise presentation handled by the professionals. However, it will be of great value if associates are taught how to arouse their customers' interest and create a desire to purchase merchandise. Associates may receive information about the products their company carries from departmental product books, magazines, catalogs hangtags, labels, care and cleaning instructions, advertising materials, and brochures.

The salesperson should present his or her products as special and treat it with great pride. Customers should be involved in handling and examining merchandise to promote likeness for them and eventually lead them to own the merchandise. As associate and customers handle and talk about the special features and characteristics, the salesperson should seize the opportunity to talk about the benefits of the merchandise. For an example, when a customer is talking about the features of boys' pants or tops, the salesperson can bring up the point of durability of the fabric and whether it is washable or not.

When the store does not have what a customer needs, he/she should suggest a similar item that is available. If there are no alternatives in the store, then the catalog could be suggested. The salesperson should be careful to select words that will encourage the customer to listen to alternatives to the customers' needs and wants. Expressions such as "May I show you—," "Have you considered—?" "Allow me to show you—."

It is not in the interest of the company that the associate will prejudge what the customers will spend. Be careful and let the customer himself decide how expensive the item he'll buy should be. Offer alternatives that are at different price points and explain the features that make the different prices. There should be a feedback or reaction from the customer to suggest that he is sure he's on the right track.

The visual department, or whatever name may be given this section of the store that presents the products to the public, takes a reasonably large share of the success of the business. It is the quality of the visual personnel that may show the quality of store presentation.

Merchandising or Product Replenishment Team

The merchandising or product replenishment team is a vital part of retail business. Their duty is to bring out merchandise to the floor from the stockroom to replace the ones that have been sold. They are to be familiar with product arrangement on a daily basis. Before the store opens to the public in the mornings, the racks and display tables and fixtures are fully stocked with merchandise. There is a need for the staff in this department to cooperate with one another and to be committed and serious at work. Workers in this sector are expected to be punctual and regular at work.

The job of the sales associate is linked to the replenishment department. The salesperson should fill in merchandise for different sections of his department as they get low on the tables and four ways on display where customers can have access to them. It therefore becomes necessary for the associate to know the department's stockroom and where different products are kept.

The stockroom workers do have significant functions in the company. A team of committed staff can help make merchandise or products easily visible and reachable for other staff members who need to work with them.

The stockrooms should be kept clean and organized. The staff in this subdivision should be faithful and committed so that the security of the room can guarantee total absence or at least reduction of shrinkage at that sector. The receiving doors are to be kept locked and secured when merchandise are not being received.

Retag, ticketed, and "chargeback" items are handled by the stockroom staff in most stores that I know. The person who handles this should complete the job quickly and return merchandise to the sale floor for the customers to access. It is very crucial for salespeople to understand this part of their job as many others because the experience in most stores is that products which otherwise would have been sold are not because they are left sitting in the stockroom where customers cannot see them.

The Loss Prevention / Security Department

The loss prevention / security department is essentially a redemption office. The staff is vested with the power to prevent and identify losses. When and if a theft incidence occurs, the staff of this department takes on the task of arresting or calling for assistance to arrest and handing over to the larger law enforcement community for investigation and punishment by alerting the staff of any suspected or real shoplifting incidents. The profit or loss made by the company is largely decided by the efficiency of the loss prevention department. The realization of a company's objectives could be enhanced by the performance of that department.

The Accounts Department

The accounts department of a retail business store is an integral part of retail. Besides ensuring that proper records of sales and returns are made, the department has an eye for error detection and control of sale activities so that incidence of shrinkage is reduced. Each register sale made is documented by the media papers and the head of accounts and the security. The department examines the paperwork at each register on a daily basis. It is the duty of this department working under the store manager to ensure that the budget is adhered to and that expenditures are coordinated properly. All sales and other monies coming into the company are monitored and accounted for by the department.

The Credit Department

The credit department is a partnership in the entire operation of the retail business. One of the ways of guaranteeing comeback customers is to persuade customers to sign up for the company's credit card that will enable them to buy as much as they desire and to come back to repeat the process. Since the major goal of retail is to satisfy the customers' needs by selling goods to them and thereby make profit for the company, it means that salespeople need to encourage customers to want to continue to buy what they need even if they do not have their own money to do so. It is becoming a necessity for survival in their workplace for salespeople to work seriously on customers to want to sign up for credit cards from the store. It has been established that customers buy more than they initially want to if they have a credit facility. Business places give monetary and material incentives to associates who are able to draw attention of people to the store products when they get them to sign up for credit cards, which will assist them to do so. Associates may get to the point of being indirectly black listed if they fail to enlist customers to the credit system. On the other hand, those who get customers in to sign for credit cards do get a lot of encouragement. They receive monetary as well as material rewards. The hardworking associates sometimes get specially commended for their efforts at store meetings. The positive side to this form of compensation is that it raises the level of enthusiasm of the salespersons. It also encourages them to continue to be loyal to the company and its programs. Salespeople who are doing well may be given a positive personality assessment and may go higher in sales ambition and future achievement's standard set for them. It generates a healthy competition among the associates while the retail business itself is being promoted.

As a many times beneficiary of these incentives, I wholeheartedly support the effort of the business as they try to recognize the efforts of their staff. I encourage the salesperson reading this book to determine to be effective in their sales career.

Often, special occasional discounts are offered to credit card holders so they can buy more goods. It is usually the practice of most companies to give extra discounts to welcome new credit card issuance partners. They get as much as 10 percent discount on all their purchases for the first time the card is open for them, and this is valid throughout that day. When the card is officially issued and mailed to the customer, an additional 10 percent discount is also offered throughout the day. Parents make use of this opportunity to do their shopping for their children's needs when and if they open a credit card. Individuals who may have been contemplating to buy huge items need to seize this opportunity to buy them and get the special discount. It is interesting to know that once the customer is led by the associate to make this decision to open a credit line, they are happy. They are happy to be fulfilling an obligation. They are glad they can meet their needs. And the associate is happy that he has met a need. Many customers are successfully won into the camp of credit card buyers, and the retail businesses continue to get a boost in their volume of sale. The credit card issuance system brings more profit to the stores than cash and check payments. So also it is more profitable if the credit card of the particular store is used over and above those of other institutions. The retail business companies may actually lose money when other forms of payments besides its credit cards are used.

The adoption of store gift cards and certificates of the mall are sales-boosting tactics. The benefits derived become the company's profit directly, and it enhances the business.

The gift card sale promotion is gaining high recognition in today's retail business. Although the pressure put on associates to get customers to sign for this type of store business is not as hard as is put on them for credit cards, companies do emphasize that associates promote the sale of gift cards. It has been observed that gift card issuance also bring in remarkable sale increase. When gift cards are used to purchase goods, the customer buys merchandise more than the value of the gift card. During religious and social festivals, associates pressurize more that customers should buy gift cards for their friends and relatives. If a customer is led to buy a gift card, he has eventually been led to bring a customer or more. By that singular action, he has also been led to bring in more business to the company. He has assisted the company to grow in trade volume.

The credit card and gift card systems are fast becoming aggressive marketing techniques in modern retail. Stores associates get extra enticements and recognition if they are able to persuade customers to open credit card accounts or buy gift cards to some loved ones.

The local credit department works directly with the store manager, but relate to the corporate credit office. Associates may have cause to refer to the corporate office. When they process credit card application online, they get approval or denial responses from the corporate office. Questions may arise over accounts information or there may be disparity in customers' accounts, and the associate may need to refer to the corporate office for answers and directions for necessary actions to be taken. The sales associate is indeed in constant relationship with the credit department.

The Custom Decorating Department

The custom decorating department is an important economic arm of the sales store. The department gives custom-made services, and it is essentially a department that does most of its work outdoors. The preparatory or planning aspect of its work is done on the computer and in the store office, and they go out to carry out the work plan. First-time home buyers and customers who need to change their home furniture and furnish their offices make use of the services of the department. Associates need to understand how this department works so they can do what they are expected to do by talking to customers and getting referrals from family and friends. The effort is usually compensated by the company. People who work in custom decorating department go out to furnish and decorate homes and give services that are measured to fit and taste as may are requested of them. In this area of operation, customer satisfaction is as important as getting customers. If a satisfactory job is done, the customer will tell other people. The quality of job done will also advertise for the company because when other people visit the home or office of the customer and he is impressed by what he sees, he will want to order a service and will in turn tell others. This chain action is a solid way of boosting company sales.

The Catalog Department

The catalog department's main function is to give the customers the service of obtaining what they want that are not available in the store. Most businesses have Web sites through which the customers/prospects can get information on the company's products that are not available in the stores. Customers' size or color of shoes and clothing may be available in the company's catalog, but may not be on the sales floor. Part of the job of the catalog department could also be done by the salespeople on the floor. They can suggest looking up an item that is not on the floor in the catalog. As long as they are company's products, they will be available in the catalog if they are current. They could be ordered directly to the customer's home or to the store. The customer will decide his or her preference. Delivery of ordered merchandise and payment for them is being handled by the catalog department. Previously bought orders may be returned to the catalog department if not found satisfactory. In some stores, this department also works as a central issuance and collection centers for register tools and many others.

The local store's catalog department work as a team with the corporate catalog department, and the sales floor order is done online to the corporate catalog office.

Catalog book sales are made at the sales floor register locations as well as at the catalog department. Like the credit card and gift card sales, catalog sales are held in high priority by the company. An associate is expected to sell the catalog books just as he is expected to do other things. The sale of catalog books is to promote the company products as they meet the needs of customers. It is the purpose of making customers' needs easy to meet that a company establishes a catalog order system. The customer does not have to come to the store to make his order. He can do so from the comfort of his home on the Internet or on the phone. He may even decide to fax his order if that's the only facility available to him. Companies try to encourage their customers to order from the catalog by sometimes offering some free issues of the catalog and selling the catalogs to them. Clearance and special sales are offered in the catalog for customer satisfaction.

Advertisement Department

Advertisement of company's products in most businesses is constantly processed. The staff in the stores should be aware of the ads being run on television and other news media. Associates should watch out for newspaper ads; it would be necessary for sales associates to be familiar with retail posters and point-of-sale displays, contests, games, clearances at seasonal, holidays, industry-related events, going out of business, and grand openings. Display accessories for retail supplies online should be a familiar feature to the staff.

Advertisements are to be watched, and attention is given to competitors' activities so that the sales associates could intensify their efforts at pushing the sales of the products of the company.

Special display of products in a given department could be an advertisement for the goods featured to be moved in quick sales.

In most businesses, the advertisement policy of the company is decided at the corporate level, and the local offices are to carry out the distribution of attention-giving posters and books. The associate is to know how important it is for him to be aware of all the forms of advertisement and their contents. This should be so because he will need to be interpreting and carrying out the contents of the advertisement on the sales floor. Besides, customers are usually up-to-date with the advertisement messages and would come to the store armed with the information. A salesperson who is not up-to-date with the same amount of information will be found wanting and may not be able to satisfy the needs of his customers. Products that are not moving as fast as has been programmed could be put on display tables or four ways that are in full glimpse of the customers. Sometimes some associates are assigned to entrances to the store or company with items or products to be advertised. The purpose is to ensure that all who come into the store will not miss the opportunity to know about it and to buy according to their needs.

Associates need to know that they are to be fully involved in all the undertakings of the store so that they can also enjoy the results of their labor.

Some companies offer their associates benefits for profit sharing. An associate incorporated into such a program has sufficient incentives to encourage him to promote the company's products and make profits.

The Personnel Department

The personnel department of the companies in their maximum strength is usually at the head office. It is at the corporate level that the policies are made and guidelines for execution formulated. The subsidiary departments are instructed about what to do

on regular basis. There is usually a representational personnel department in every store location. Computers are made available for entries of information that the home office can work with. Application forms for employment are completed online and the local stores select their staff as needed. Processing of appointments is done online by the local personnel office. Relevant interactive procedures are maintained by the personnel department. The welfare of the staff is taken up by the personnel department. Some companies make different arrangements about the allocation of functions, but in the most part, the personnel or human resources office overlook this area of staff needs.

Insurance and medical matters form part of the responsibility of the personnel or human resources department. Associates are encouraged to sign up for programs that allow their company to assist them in their health maintenance.

Advice is given to the salespersons as needed, and questions about administrative and personnel matters could be asked to the supervisor for their department. One thing affects the other. If associates have a clear picture of how they need to go about getting the information they need and getting the services they require, they are likely to be in good shape for efficient performance of their duties to the customers.

The position of the store manager is a key position of responsibilities. It is the uttermost hierarchy at the retail store. A high degree of monitoring and controlling is required of this chief executive. He is not only expected to be alert to the movement of people and goods, but he must always be aware of the needs of the customers and visitors, contractors, and staff. He oversees the proper movement of incoming (stock) and outgoing (merchandise for sale, charge) transactions.

He is the corporate office representative in the store. It is through him that the company policy, regulations, and expectations are conveyed to the staff, and feedback is given to the corporate office.

A positive, understanding, and friendly store manager would effectively move his staff to perform with maximum efficiency and to make profit and build sales. In like manner, he is expected to sensitize the corporate office to good appreciation and reward to deserving members of staff.

It is because of the complex nature of retail that the staff of the company should study and understand the network. It is the reason for them to be taught what they are expected to do in relation to others in the department where they work and to those in other departments.

Customer Service

This is the most important factor of retail business. It is so important that stores display vivid signs of the customer service centers so that customers can have easy access to the associates who can answer questions and solve their problems.

The functions of building and setting up of a store and the decision on products are centered on customers. All services should indeed be focused on the customers.

The location of a store may determine the status or categories of customers that the business will attract because mobility may be restricted. In a developed society such as the United States of America where there is easy transportation, there may not be any hard-and-fast rule about a concentration of particular group of people or products for sale. People are free to visit and shop anywhere they like.

The fact that a retail store can attract different kinds of people is the same reason to expect different behavioral patterns and different temperaments. Some customers will be polite, friendly, and cooperative, and some are not. A salesperson is expected to be able to accommodate these various groups of people and be friendly, polite, and meet customers with sincere smile. If the customer behaves nastily, the salesperson should not react equally, but should be positive and polite. It should be remembered that the customer has come to be served. He has come to fulfill a need and has considered the particular store to be capable of taking care of that need. He is therefore to be taken as always being right. For the company to stay in business, quality service should be given at all times. Since purchasing or buying is dictated by emotions, a salesperson should be careful not to exhibit negative emotions that will translate into negative emotions to the customers and prospects. The sales associate's words and actions are being observed by the prospects and customers and are filed away for later use to help them decide whether to trust you or not to do business with you. Any slackness or inappropriate behavior on the part of any of the associates may work against the achievement of the company's purpose for being in business.

The competitive nature of business is also a reason for good customer service. Unique and common services need to be offered. If different business names are set up to meet similar needs, what store A offers, store B needs to sell or work toward offering. If a store offers common services, the chances are that customers might have it on the list of shops they patronize. In the event that a store offers more than others offer, the possibility may be that it will serve more customers than the others. The extras may be in the form of products for sale, quality of staff, and floor presentation of products. Whenever additional services are offered, the customer service associate is expected to do more. It is not often that added responsibilities come with pay increase. But any store that remunerates associates adequately is probably seriously aware of the importance of people in the development of a business.

The customer service personnel in retail have opportunities for learning new things and developing skills in human relations. They need to be willing to adjust and survive in a competitive world. Some salespersons may be interested in making a profession of it, and others may want to do their own sale business when they quit regular employment.

Like the authors whose works I have earlier reviewed in this book, I believe that salespeople should have the knowledge of their products. While this may not be the most important thing to know, it will help him in his sales promotion if he knows his products, the advantages of such products to his customers, and the importance of leading the customers to appreciate the advantages.

The customer may want to know the properties from which a product is made. Even though the customer may have been able to read this from the label, the associate should be in the position to comfortably tell the customer the obvious. The knowledge of the advantages of the associate's product over a similar one sold by the competitor is a plus for the company. The retail associate should have similar knowledge that he has of his company's products, about his company's competitors, and identify the advantages and disadvantages that his company's products have over others. He should know the company's strengths and capitalize on them. The associate's knowledge will enable him to lead the customer to opt for the associate's company's products.

Why an associate should have a broad knowledge of the interrelationship of the departments in his company is mainly because of the advantages this will bring to the volume of sales. The knowledge of this network of relationship will translate into useful information to the customer. For an example, a customer or a prospect may need to purchase a company product from a different department from that of the retail person.

When approached for help, a retail person should be able to guide the customer to the appropriate section of the store where he can locate the item. Sometimes this may require the associate physically taking the customer to where the product could be obtained.

A customer who has just purchased a dress may also want a pair of shoes to go with it and may require the assistance of an associate to do so. The associate should be able to do consultative selling by color and style of shoes that will coordinate the dress. Associates who work in the clothing department are to have knowledge of colors and on how to arrange their four ways or racks and tables in a way that will meet the color scheme. Arrangement and sizing should be an additional skill to be acquired in this regard. Apart from the advantages of the knowledge of the associate for his store, his own life could be enhanced by the awareness that some colors go together and some do not.

Add-on sales like jewels, hats, and handbags to go with the new dress should be suggested to the customer by the retail associate. Even perfume wearing could be added to the list of suggestions in this area.

The salesperson should be able to know the needs of his customers and be prepared to build ideas for them and offer solutions to their problems.

From the experience I have personally gathered from the sales floor, I know that the salesperson has many open opportunities to make a sale for his company. Some customers come to the store with no idea whatsoever of how to get what they need. They have little knowledge of the size of clothes that fit well or the style that fits their shape and size. Some come with a list of requirements on their children's school list, but that's about all they know about such lists. This kind of situation opens a wide door of opportunities for the associate to tap on. Sometimes a customer knows about ongoing clearance sales, and he appears without a plan for what he wants to buy. If the associate is aware of this gold mine opportunity to sell, he can lead the customer to buy a lot to meet some of his needs.

I believe that the human resources department of companies need to monitor more closely the activities of their associates in the field of add-on sales and reward associates who bring in additional business to their company and find ways of encouraging those who are not doing enough in that area to do so.

Kimball identified the need for a salesperson to know his limitations and, in the light of all these, develop the strategy and tactics that give his company the greatest possibility of winning. (1994) This, he also found, might mean that retail persons need to be keeping up with all the industry and trade associations and getting exposure for the retail persons and their company in the industry and trade journals. Retail associates are to keep track of legislation and regulation as they affect their businesses. They should be aware of product alternatives and innovations from domestic and foreign competition and know the prevalent feel for economic and financial conditions that may impact the whole industry. (Kimball, 1994)

The works of the authors I have earlier reviewed in this book emphasize that the associate should learn to listen to the customer. My sales experience confirms that you listen to the customer and you know what to do to help him and you consequently make a sale. You do not listen to him and you do most of the talking and you lose the chance to meet those needs. It is important to be a good listener. It is helpful to use leading questions to get the customer to open up and let you know his needs, and you can help him. Allowing the customer to talk while you listen encourages him to trust you and allow you to introduce your products, which if purchased may lead to continuous business.

All the expectations expressed in the foregoing paragraph may seem overwhelming to a retail associate especially when we consider the limited skills imparted to them at recruitment training session. The magnitude of the requirements may not even encourage the associate to easily yield to improvement when the inadequate incentives given are put on the balance. But they are qualities and abilities that are needed in people who are employed to promote sales and improve profits.

Later in this book, these aspects will be more fully discussed when we examine the hiring system of retail employers and the quality and limited training given to the associates at the time of hiring.

Perhaps one of the most important areas of retail that should be very constantly pursued is shrinkage prevention.

Chapter 3

Prevention of Shrinkage

This area of company operation is vital to our consideration on sales. All of the efforts of selling and making gains may be lost without cautious efforts to control shrinkage. A company's poster advises that one way of preventing shrinkage is to make the customers a sale offer that they cannot refuse. Another thing the salespeople could do is to help keep organized criminals out of the stores. Organized crime groups are said to be hard to spot. Some of them try to distract other people while their buddies have opportunity to steal merchandise. The salesperson should be aware of their tactics so they are not intimidated and can stay alert and provide good customer service. An associate should call for help if he feels he is being distracted. Also if he sees any of his company's products for sale at the flea market or at any unauthorized store, he should call the loss prevention hotline (J.C. Penney Company Inc. posters, *The University of Shrinkage,* 2005) Most companies operate the hotline system. The *Hotline* is an anonymous report of any suspected wrongdoing in the company or store so they could be immediately stopped or minimized.

To put up a winning fight against the shoplifter, the employees should work as a team. Creation of awareness of merchandise location in the departments is a good tool to be used in reducing shrinkage. Merchandise should have the correct bar code to scan for the right prices. Sometimes products' tags are missing due to wrong handling. Sometimes the wrong tags get on products either by design of frivolous people or by error. Whatever may be responsible, the associate should be aware of such errors and call the attention of his supervisor to it so that the right price could appear on the product's price tag. Paying attention to details and reporting pricing discrepancies and UPCs (Universal Product Codes) that don't scan are effective ways of reducing errors and minimizing shrinkage.

For an example, for whatever reason, an item that should cost more can carry the tag of an item that costs far less. When a customer takes that item to the register, he is expecting a bill of that value. A vigilant associate who knows his products well will be able to detect that the item should cost more than the tag shows, and he can prevent a loss.

Regular inventory and periodic auditing should be done to keep track of any failures so they could be corrected on time.

Prevention of theft could be buttressed by the use of ink tags. This may deter thieves from making away with store items. The ink tag device is expected to set off an alarm when the product tries to go out illegally. When the alarm sounds, the security people will accost the carrier of the product, and legal issues could arise. The important thing for the company is that a theft has been prevented and so is loss prevented.

Accuracy in store operation could be pursued by properly ticketing merchandise and constantly checking to see that goods remain tagged properly. When selling a gift card, a salesperson should ensure that the gift card number matches the one showing on the screen. If it does not, a supervisor or a manager should be called. That manager or supervisor will keep the compromised card and assist the customer politely with another gift card. The compromised card will then be turned to the loss prevention department for their follow-up review. (J.C.Penney Company poster, *Instructions on Sale of Gift Cards*, 2005)

Associates should especially be encouraged to look for "I bit back" situations as they straighten and arrange their store. "I bit back" situations are opportunities to find company's goods that are about to be stolen and to retrieve them for the company. Sometimes someone whose intention is to steal may come into a store and rake up clothes from the four-way (racks) or pile-up products that he may be planning on taking away when no one is looking. A constant vigilance of the associates on that floor and in that section is likely to burst that evil plan. Sometimes items are moved out of place and hidden for the purpose of walking away with them later. Shoes may be found in the four ways of the clothing department. A box of jewels may be found among baby stuff. Things from one department may be piled up in another department. All of these oddities are deliberate attempts to steal, and they should be prevented by being vigilant.

Receiving doors of the stores should be locked and secured when merchandise is not being received so as to prevent invasion of unwanted persons.

An associate should know and understand the policies and procedures of the company and should not be overwhelmed by them. If there is any area that he does not understand, he should ask the supervisor or the manager.

By and large, effective shrinkage requires retail associates' great customer service and alertness. An associate should fight crime with a smile. A quick recognition of a customer as he comes in the door or as he starts to look around the store will show the people that you are watching them.

It will do a number of other good things. It will likely portray the store as friendly and accommodating, and that kind of feeling is good for the company. The good impression created for the company may produce comeback customers and prospects. The stranger in the store with an ulterior motive will likely be discouraged from getting away with the merchandise and may want to pay for it or at least not steal it.

Selling is a science, based on documented principles that can be learned by anyone of average intelligence. As a science, it has "an underlying view of human nature, a concomitant set of principles that are learned by study and experimentations to daily life." (Brooks, 1992, 47)

Chapter 4

Hiring And Staff Training

Since selling is a principle-based art, the people who will be employed to sell should understand sound philosophically based principles, which are timeless. Unlike techniques that have short-range goals, principles will always apply.

Brooks recognized that the practical application of these principles is that the staff or people who will be employed to sell should always make sure they fulfill the customers' needs by giving them enough value to more than justify what they invest. (Brooks, 1992, 67)

The questions to be asked at this point are the following:

> Do the human resources or the personnel departments of companies consider that they should hire people who have demonstrated potentials relevant to their companies' expectation?
>
> Do they just offer jobs to those who will accept their salary offers as they are?
>
> Do the people themselves think respectfully of retail?
>
> Do the applicants for the sales position think respectfully of the profession themselves?
>
> Do the employers know if they will treat the employees with respect after hiring the people?

My observations and experience have identified the need for employers of retail people to have a laid down policy on remuneration and hire people who have the basic educational qualification and who they will train formally and on the job. Most of the people who apply to their organizations for a job are people who, for one reason or another, are in dire need of some income, who will take their employment as a temporary measure while they look out for better employment opportunities. If and when the people are hired, they are given what amounts to scanty training. That training given is pertinent to their company's needs and is not centrally conceptual to training. Most human resource departments develop scanty pages of training brochures, sometimes as few as four to five pages. The contents of the notes are usually about what the associate is expected to do at the register and how it is to be operated. Sometimes they get as close as to getting information on the ways of greeting prospects and customers when they get to the store. There is an agreement by all the writers whose books I reviewed that there is basically no training given to salespeople on the skills they need to sell.

Selling, it is agreed, is a complex profession; and it requires skills. Training is to be given to every hired staff, and continuous training should be programmed. Organizations do experience changes, and the staff should be initiated into the restructuring processes. The philosophical principles of selling and their practical applications need be taught.

The better qualified and experienced the employees are, the better the quality of performance and the higher the possibility of good profit for the companies. The intellectual capability is an asset that may assist the associate in making fairly good judgments. There may be guidelines to which strict adherence is required, but on-the-spot decisions, which may not fit squarely within a guideline, are not uncommon in the day-to-day actions of an associate. Even though there may be graded categories of staff such as the managers, supervisors, and merchandisers, there are still instances where the customer is shopping in a hurry, or he is naturally impatient and may decide not to wait for a supervisor or a manager to come and fix the problem.

The nature of the business may be a factor to consider in hiring and paying staff. Whatever is the situation, there can be no argument against paying commensurately a person who is expected to perform well.

Training should be given on personal appearance and dressing, which should stand out although not exorbitantly. Retail staff should be helped to understand that they need to, more or less, sell themselves before they sell to the customer, and so they should give a good impression of themselves as well as the company they represent.

Included in the "self-sale" package are voice pitch, eye contact, standing posture, and manners. Salespeople are to be taught to speak clearly and naturally. They should stand in a businesslike manner and not casually. They are to remember their good manners, be courteous, and polite even if the customer acts negatively.

Andrews said that a salesperson should know that to be a success as a salesman, a person has to be a success first. She further recommended that salespeople are to be educated in the procedure of "opening and closing" a sale.(1986) "Opening a sale" is probably the hardest part of making a sale. To sell, the salesperson has to plunge right in, remember everything he or she knows about the product, and use flexible strategy in approaching the customer as he leads him to make a choice of product. Salespeople are to be taught how to assist customers in selecting the right merchandise. One way is to ask "open-ended" questions in a friendly way to establish their wants and needs. Open-ended questions such as *what*, *why*, *how*, and *tell me* are used to initiate a customer in opening up his wants and needs.

Open questions like these encourage an easy flow of information and can lead to a great deal of sales. A good listener is likely to be a good learner. Therefore, salespersons are to listen as customers tell their needs.

The body language of the salesperson should be positive so that he can attract positive reaction from the customer. The salesperson should be aware of this so he can be alert to the customer's signs and adjust to needs as necessary.

The purpose of opening the sale is to begin an agreement with the customer to buy the merchandise. Through the gestures and questions described in the foregoing paragraphs, the customer proceeds to buy the merchandise, and the sale is closed. Closing statements that may be used are as follows:

> "Would you prefer the green shirt to the blue _____ [any company
> products' name could fit into the question]?"
> "Would you like me to bring the smaller size, the bigger size, or the medium
> size?"

If the company that the sales representative works with operates a credit card system, he may say, "May I put this on your [insert relevant company] card?"

The salesperson should feel confident in asking the customers and prospects for these sales. While an associate may not necessarily make a sale with a customer, there are chances that he can increase his chances of sales and of customers.

A closed sale is therefore a possible success for the salesperson who has applied all the procedures of positive selling.

Sale Register Operation

Most businesses operate with the use of the register. More often than not, salespeople find themselves operating the sale register. Register training is therefore a necessary part of orientation to the company where the salesperson will work. From experience and information gathered from salespeople, register operation training is not done in depth. As soon as the hired person can demonstrate superficial ability to operate the register, he or she is thrown on the floor to work. He or she is left to the other associates in the department to, more or less, fill in the gaps.

The operation of the sale register should be smooth, and the posture assumed at the register should be professional. The customer is at close quarters with the sales associate while what he or she sees at that distance could encourage him to come back or discourage him or her from doing further business with the company. The correct sale prices should be entered in cases where price adjustments are necessary. Mistakes made at the register may bring remarkable loss to the company. Since the major focus of retail like any business endeavor is to make profit, it is my desire that companies will emphasize the register (which is the point of service) training in all sales floor staff hiring procedure.

The operation of the register requires a basic knowledge of the use of the computer, and I believe that a salesperson should be put through the basic principles of the computer before he is hired. This is becoming more relevant as the computer becomes more sophisticated. The lack of or deficiency of knowledge in accurate use of the computer may have adverse effects on the business. In the first instance, a sales associate who will be struggling with the operation of the register will delay the customer he is serving at a particular moment. He will in turn keep a queue long and customers waiting in line. Customers and prospects may become inpatient and may leave their merchandise and go to other stores to buy what they need. The same customer will leave either verbally complaining of how slow the workers are in that company or going out to say to people what he may have been quiet about. Either of these reactions is a portrayer of poor customer service, which is poor business. The company should take the matter of register operation seriously and should just not push someone there for filling a usual missing gap.

If well managed, register performance will enhance good customer relations and great customer service.

Handling Returns

The handling of returns is another vital area of a company's business. As simple as the operation may sound to be, it is one area where great customer service is needed. A customer who brings an item back to the store of purchase expects either of two things in return. He expects to get exchange or get a refund for the returned items. Sometimes these may not come as easily as the customer expects. How the situation that may arise is handled will be determined by the kind of service the associate can offer.

The policy of many retail businesses allows the customers to return unwanted goods. Some give specific period of time within which refund will be made. Others are open, and customers may come at their convenience. Some companies insist that the products to be returned should be accompanied with an original receipt, or the company will return at the current purchase value only. This may not really be an issue with some companies. While some companies still accommodate returns of already worn clothes or used items, some will not take back goods that are not brought back in their original condition at purchase.

Customers should be free to return products if they choose. The salesperson should do all he can to encourage the customers to come back. Returns should always be handled with a smile and a pleasant attitude no matter what the company return policy is. Customers may go to the extent of being hostile if for any reason their refund is reduced in value at purchase or if it appears their return procedure is delayed or made difficult. The retail associates handling a return should always remember that the company's reputation is in their hands. They should also remember that each return brings an opportunity for opening and closing of sales. They can ask the customer who is returning a product if he would like a different color or a different size or a different brand. Suggest a variety of choices, which will make the customer settle with an exchange of products rather than a return of goods. If the customer is not happy with the choices suggested in the store or company, the associate may suggest looking in the catalog for a different style or something different entirely.

Most companies would allow customers to return goods in any of their stores nationwide. Again, some companies would insist on the presentation of a receipt of purchase before the goods could be accepted for return. Some others would let things go by if a receipt could not be presented for the transaction.

Most companies have special codes that are used for controlling fraudulent returns. There are people who may have stolen company products and later turn round to return them as "returns" without receipts. Some people bring products from a branch of the company and go either outside the state or the geographical area from where they might have to return the possibly stolen goods in another geographical location. Such stolen goods are coded, and when there is an attempt to return them, the computer brings out the code. At that stage, the associate should call a supervisor or a manager who will take the necessary steps to deal with the matter. Shrinkage could be prevented or reduced if an associate is sufficiently knowledgeable in the proper return process. Goods returned should be entered into the computer system by comparing the returned items with the price given on the day of purchase and entering that value against the correct numbers returned. There have been cases where relatively new salespersons have given customers the total value on the receipt of all purchases whereas they were just returning a few items on that receipt. When questioned why he did that, an associate replied that he was returning as the receipt showed and that he had been trained to return according to the receipt. If the value on the receipt is $200 and the actual items brought for return are worth $25, that singular error of return had brought the company a $175 shortage. That kind of mistake would be continued unless proper training was given to the associate.

Training is required in handling returns so that salespeople may acquire skills that will help them to treat returns of goods accurately. A salesperson should be able to help arrive at the correct amount of refund. For an instance, if a product is being returned without a receipt and the computer memory of that product because it had been sold a long time, the salesperson should be able to help arrive at the correct amount of refund by conferring with his supervisor. Organizations do many great things to promote their businesses. One of such is putting their goods on clearance sales. An item that is purchased when a clearance sale is on may be returned when no sales are on without the clearance mark on it. A customer without a receipt may expect to get the refund at current terms when actually he has paid less for the goods. There should always be a careful look at the price tag, and if it has been taken off, the associate should look at the price on a similar tag to determine the actual amount of refund. Establishing that the product, which is being brought as a return, is the company's product is of vital importance because it might contribute to shrinkage volume of the company. Payment of money to a customer who has not at any time brought in such money may be a loss to the company.

A well-performed refund act may well be a good way of reducing shrinkage.

Chapter 5

Challenges in Retail And How to Deal with Them

Whatever it may be that we do in life, we should always be prepared to face challenges. It is the kind of preparation that we make that will prepare us for success and victory or failure. The retail business is full of challenges, and an associate worth his salt must know what these challenges are and how he will face them and succeed.

Objections from Customers

Price objection is one of the challenges of the business. Customers may not always accept the price tag value or the quality of the company's goods. They may not even like the colors of merchandise or the way the company has presented them. Whatever type of objections may be raised by the customer, the salesperson is to anticipate them from the customers and should be prepared to accept and not deny them. Sometimes the objections will be nonverbal. The salesperson needs to understand the customer's viewpoint, but should not agree or disagree. Rather than consent to either of these, he may make statements such as follows:

"I understand."

"I see!"

"I appreciate that."

"That's fine."

If price objections are raised, the associate should stress the quality and value, review benefits, and help the customers see how this may relate to their wants and needs. The associate could talk about investment buying and on how the features of the products or merchandise differ from the less expensive items. An associate should not take the objection experience personally even if the customer presents it as such. The salesperson should always remember that "it is the service the company is not obliged to give that people value most." (*J.C. Penney Company Inc. Manual*, 1934)

Jolles considered objection by customers as a challenge to the retail business. He said that customers might be objecting to various things such as fear of change, which may be in the form of the price, store arrangement, or they may feel they have no need of the product. Some customers object to the aggressiveness of the sales associate, and some have no reasons for their objection. Whatever may be the nature or reasons for the objection, Jolles viewed objection as crucial to the success in selling.(1998) He recommended that the objections are first to be clarified by asking clarification questions and avoiding answering the wrong objections. Furthermore, he said that the salesperson should avoid sounding confrontational and appearing to be in a rush to get rid of the customer.

He advised the salesperson to "buy himself time, shorten his talking so as not to give the objection credibility and needs to gracefully assist the customer out of his predicament and acknowledge his objection." (1998, 285) Jolles summarized his recommendation with the Pareto principle which" in problem solving basically teaches you to separate the trivial many from the vital few, prepare for the vital few objections, and welcome them with open arms." (1998, 301)

Brooks acknowledged objection as "a challenge in selling." He advised salespersons to identify objections and isolate obstacles that may cause a prospect not to make a buying decision. (1992, 246)

Andrews saw rejection as a challenge, and she thought it is something that a salesperson needs to learn to live with. She suggested that a salesperson should get involved with people and "the more involved with people the more he gets to know his customers and the more he can sell." (1986, 53)

Mitchell said that real objections by customers is a challenge to selling and that the salesperson can handle it as an open invitation to satisfy the buyer's urge, and if the salesperson will help those who raise the objection, he will sell his products or services. Mitchell recommended that the salesperson does not interfere with objections so he will not alienate his customers. He said that customers are to be assisted to open up to the salesperson and articulate his reasons for objections. He said that the salesperson may use open-ended question such as, "You must have a reason for saying that, may I ask what it is?" This type of question, Mitchell submitted, may elicit a yes reply, and that may assist the customer to open up to the salesperson and create positive forces that will move the decision toward the sale. (1991, 157-158)

Kimball said that customer's objections should be anticipated and should be seen by the salesperson as an opportunity to make a friend. He saw objection as an opportunity for the salesperson to encourage the customer to talk and for the salesperson to provide guiding questions that will help the customer to seek the benefits of the company's products. Kimball suggested the use of "escalator technique," which will help the customer to appreciate the product give an affirmative response and build an agreement. He suggested a tag on a question as follows: "This product is rated tops by Consumer Reports. That says a lot about its quality, doesn't it?" (1996, 174-175)

Girard found that confidence and courage are needed by the salesperson to overcome challenges in selling. He said there needs to be" a plan of steps and strategies to knock down the difficulties successfully." (1995, 35)

LeBoeuf said that handling challenges of sale could be done successfully when salespeople know that they will be tested, but they are not to give up. He admonished salespeople to see setbacks and hard times as "the seed of future victories and should be smart enough to look for them." (1996, 208)

Handling Complexities of Human Behavior

It stands to reason that an associate or any person who will be dealing with people should understand people and how they may react to situations especially when their personal interest is at stake. Salespeople need to be helped by the company to know what people are likely to be and how that may be handled to the advantage of the consumer as well as the company. Clienteles of retail consist of different classes of people, and it is amazing to know how much of the human nature and character could be observed in the sales procedure. Training in human relations skills need to be given when a salesperson is hired and during further staff development programs of the company.

Change As It May Affect Selling

Organizations need to teach their staff the concept of change and on how to take advantage of the changes that may come. Brooks identified hard economic times as a challenge in selling. He said, "War may ravage nations and have international dimensions." (1992, x) A salesperson is to equip himself with the knowledge of the change and on how it can affect the business of his company. As necessary, skills and motivation should be developed to enable salespeople become committed to the work he does and to meet the challenges posed by the change. Sales training is to be directed to the goals of the organization, and it is to be suited to the new demands that the changes may bring so that it can be relevant to the needs of the businesses and the organizations. The salesperson needs to be able to use questions to make value connections and find out what the customer wants most. Jolles agreed that changes do come in the way of businesses, and that change is generally feared by people. He said there are a number of ways in which changes may occur. "One of them may be due to technological advancement which may cause changes in the way products are packaged and which may not be acceptable to people." (1998, 277) It is the challenge to which the company must find solution for product acceptability if it will survive the change. This type of challenge, as others, requires adequate training of the associate who will be the direct contact of people caught in the challenge of change. Linked to the challenges of change is the challenge of goal setting. Associates are to be carried along with the goal-setting program of the organization. Goals are recommended to be flexible to allow a change to be made when there is need for it.

Goal Setting Could Be a Challenge

Realistic goal setting could be a problem in sales. Companies may set goals for associate salespeople to accomplish within a period of time that is not possible. Some associates may be too overwhelmed by the constant demands on them that they do unorthodox things to achieve their goals, and in some cases, they may not even have the courage to perform. Jolles observed that salespersons that do not excel might be ultimately fired while those who can excel are rewarded. The danger in this, according to him, is that the pressure tends to produce number at the expense of ethics.(1998, 11) Girard recommended that there needs to be clearly defined, realistic, achievable goals whether short range, long range, or both, whether minor or major. He further recommended that there be a way of measuring the progress made so that there will be a way of knowing how the business is faring. (1995) Salespeople are to be poised to take positive risks according to the dictates of the company. Brooks found that some organizations find it difficult to focus on their goals and suggested that salespersons be guided to have the ability to focus and maintain a sense of targeted direction in the face of obstacles. He suggested that short-range and long-term goals that will be set are to be those that can be achieved "with current resources and the ability of the staff to perform within a specified time frame." (1992, 230)

Boredom And Frustration

Even though there may appear to be many activities surrounding the business of retail, boredom and frustration could be a challenge for the salesperson. Some of the reasons for boredom and frustration could be worry about achieving set targets, lack of interest in the job or inability to perform on the job, and inadequate compensation for the work of the salespeople.

In addressing this area of challenge, Andrews advised salespeople not to be worried, but be excited about long-term goals and be ready to adjust upward or otherwise as the situation may demand. Furthermore, she said selling is about people more than anything else, and that a salesperson should engage in selling what he likes himself. She said to suppress boredom and pressure the salesman should employ the use of all his five senses when he sells. (1986)

The salesperson needs to have some diversionary activity to make room for fun when he sells. If, for an example, he is selling an automobile or suitcases, he can engage in discussion with the customer along the line of trips they are planning or may be embarking upon later. Then you get the customer talking and open the door for a variety of interesting information from the customer.

This, however, needs to be cautioned so the salesperson does not get derailed from the focus on the customer and the business before him.

Effective Use of Time

The salesperson has to contend with time and needs to be concerned about effective use of it by making every moment count toward him. In all cases, the salesperson should follow the customer's mood. Some customers and prospects are just in the store to look for something briefly and may check out of the store before any associate can reach them.

Any serious attempt to establish a rapport with them may meet with resentment. Other customers may be relaxed at their shopping time and may have the entire family with them. Such a situation may create a good opportunity for the sales associate to meet a variety of needs and make sales for his employer.

Brooks found that having a good sense of timing is very important in selling. He said that a salesperson is to know when to close a sale, at what time he is to talk, and when he should listen to the customer. (1992) Proper action needs to be taken so that a salesperson could catch the sale. Andrews saw the right use of time as a challenge in selling. She suggested that the salesperson should make good use of the time and know when it is time to help the buyer to buy what he sells or use the service he has to offer. (1986)

LeBoeuf identified effective use of time as a challenge of selling. He stated that what salespeople actually sell is "time," regardless of their product or service. He advised salespeople to "get specific goals and priorities and make adjustments along the way as necessary." (1996, 139) In LeBoeuf's submission, "good time management" actually means, "doing important things first." (1996)

Rogak recommended that salespeople be trained to effectively manage their time to allow 10-20 percent more time to complete a project than they normally would so that working at breakneck speed will be prevented. (1999)

Crisis Management And No-Sale Situations

There is need for demonstration of courage and confidence in overcoming the challenges that may be posed by crisis and "no sale" occurrence in business. Mitchell's panacea for these situations was preventive. He said that they could. He said that many potential crises could be cut off when goals are set and prioritized and a plan is well laid out for flexibility. (1991) Kimball suggested that a "contingency" plan should be prepared to handle what can go wrong and the steps to be taken in advance of things going out of place. (1975)

There are occasions when businesses do not make sales either because of negative weather conditions or because customers who come in just do not buy for various reasons. Kimball's opinion was that when no sales happen, salespersons are to learn from the experience and incorporate such into their future dealing with customers when they buy. The salesperson's involvement with the customer should be a continuous practice. Sometimes when customers come in and no sales are made, it could be because salespersons lack the skills of questioning or negotiating, overcoming objections, and closing or that the skills have not been effectively applied. Kimball suggested that each no-sale and crisis experience should be critiqued by the salespersons and their organization. The information that they obtain from the exercise should be used as strength and courage to face future sales. (1975)

Rather than be disgusted by the crisis and "no business" situation that they may find themselves, the salespersons should thank the customers for their time in coming to shop and encourage them to be back. "Thank you for your time, and please come back to see us" is a better parting gesture than a negative body language or sealed lips.

Facing Competitions

Competition is a human reality, which begins right in the home and extends to the school, the workplace, and the entire sphere of human activities. It is an art to be learned and accepted. It is to be known that being in competition requires eternal vigilance and constant improvement of our skills, actions, and ways of life. Being in business competition requires double efforts of survival tactics because competition is rising by the day. Products are being improved upon and offered at less prices; services are made more affordable and efficiently. The Internet is another world of open competition of products and services. Most companies are designing activities that encourage competition and which will also help salespersons to work hard toward achievement of goals that will in turn benefit the companies. Salespersons are to align themselves with the company's marketing strategy.

Some authors, in dealing with this area of challenge, recommended that the salespeople should know their competitors as well as the prospects and use the information to plan their survival tactics. Others said companies need to know their competitors, but do not have to concentrate on that, but rather try and come up with unique ideas of their own and plan on them.

Rogak suggested that companies discover facts about the businesses they are in competition with and learn the details about their own businesses. Rogak said that focusing on what sets the businesses apart from the competition could be an invaluable tool to work with from the customers' and prospects' eyes. He recommended that businesspeople are to "look for things or services they can offer the lovers of their products and services which will make them want to visit their stores and not the others." (1996, 140)

LeBoeuf thought that a better idea is not to compete, but to create. This, to him, offered a better alternative than knowing the competitors. He suggested that salespersons should "use their imagination to think up new products and services that make the competitor's existing ones obsolete and find faster, cheaper, and better ways to get things done and staying close to the customer as creative partners." (1996, 135)

A high quality of service is necessary in the face of competition. Stores associates who understand the business of their company and who have been trained in the skills of customer service are of immense value in the competitive business. A well-organized, carefully presented store would have greater appeal than one that does not follow any careful selection of colors and goods.

The staff remuneration that adequately rewards the efforts of skilled staff is more likely to encourage staff to stay for a long time in the establishment and continue to work fruitfully. However, businesses that do not adequately cater for their associates are likely to encounter a large turnover of staff, and this cannot augur well for the growth of the organization.

Generous condition of service, which may encourage staff to stay with the employers even until retirement, is recommended as a favorable condition for competitive trade and survival. Some stores have opportunities for employees to participate in part ownership package of the company. This may require a monthly or bimonthly contribution from employees that could be deducted from the payroll. The feeling of belongingness is a feeling that could translate into absolute loyalty and maximum effort from the employees. This is the level the company should attain, and there does not seem to be anything too much to do for the sales associates to reach and also to maintain.

Effective Use of Questions

Mitchell established that the choice of good questioning technique could be a problem in selling. The salesperson, according to him, needs to use language in an appropriate way as he relates to the customer. He recommended that the salesperson should use the language his customer will understand and be aware that whoever asks questions controls the conversation.

He said that the open- and closed-ended questions have their appropriate use in sales such as when a customer talks endlessly and needs to be guided to focus on the value of their product or service. (1991)

Andrews said that the salesperson should always prepare for the customer's questions and have his answers ready. She added that the customer's question thinking is to be done for him. Andrews discovered that the customer's trust in the salesperson may depend on how well the questions are managed. (1986)

The salesperson can make value connections of his products and services with his customer if he can create the right question in the right way to guide his customer to want the benefits of his products or service.

Hiring And Training Procedure

All the aforementioned challenges to retail could be successfully handled and success made of businesses if there are trained people to carry out the well laid-out plan of an organization. Whether we talk about changes or use of effective sales tools such as questions and good customer service, we need to consider people who will carry out the desirable functions of business. The issue then becomes what type of people, and the answer is "carefully selected and well-trained people."

Good staffing is essential to good retail business. The better-educated, experienced salespeople a company hires, the more likely better the results of sales. Very articulate, intelligent salespeople can make decisions that could bring profit to the organization and save it a lot of money.

Jolles saw the need to teach salespeople the theory and practice of selling and for trainers to "localize the selling process and make their sales people familiar with the methods of persuasion which is very critical to sales persons' success." (1998, 3) Furthermore, Jolles said that there should be a standard measurement with a consistent system of hiring salespeople selectively.

LeBoeuf found that the knowledge of the art of learning and the art of being an effective communicator are accomplishments that organizations of retail need to give their sales staff. He said, "Most successful people make the best decisions because they are the best informed and those people get good information from being avid learners and are able to effectively influence others to do what they want." (1996, 66)

Large successful companies like Motorola require that all employees spend at least 5 percent of their time on the job in training and learning new skills. LeBoeuf believed that any other businesses that invest a similar degree of time on staff development would likely get the same amount of payoff (1996). Authors of books on sales training agree with Girard that "businesses that rise up will stay up if they take the pains of giving their sales people sound preparation, knowledge, skills, the ability to set reasonable goals, sound judgment, determination and continuous self development." (1995, 7)

Training of staff in all applications remains the clinger to effective and successful retail trade, and it is one reason that it has attracted some emphasis in this book. It is hoped that industries will find it so important that they will "revolutionize" their staff-training program.

Chapter 6

Excitements And Incentives in the Retail World

Excitements In the Retail Business

In the foregoing discussions, the sales associate is put through some rigorous exercises of skill assimilation and imparting of them in his profession. He is given a number of expectations on the trade, and some demands are made on him to act according to the requirements so that the company can achieve its goals. All of these "should be" demands may sometimes be intimidating. They may even sound discouraging to a prospective salesperson. But they need not be. The world of retail is full of excitements. It is not full of boredom and tight schedule as it may appear to be. It could be a fun-filled, rewarding world.

Each workday brings a different kind of thrill and activities. New people show up in the store or company. While some come to buy, others come to make inquiries and to window-shop. There are also different kinds of people and nationalities and colors. There may not be better opportunities to learn about people generally than on the sales floor. Without necessarily traveling out of your geographical location, you could know what may be happening in some distant countries. What you have read from books become real and practical as the sales-floor experience presents them to you.

I am always excited to meet people and wait on them. I particularly enjoy discussing with customers and prospects as I walk the floor in the course of my duty. I have had the practical experience of what most of the authors whose work I have reviewed have said regarding the positive customer's response when they meet listening associates. I have listened to a number of customers who have volunteered information that are really personal to them. Perhaps a lead an associate has given about a particular color or style of dress would lead the customer to tell about his marriage or the color taste of her grandmother. Even though you may have just met them, they become so familiar that they may qualify for a friend. Such is the unlimited opportunities of retail.

The retail world is a world of activities. The activities come in various forms and colors. Sales promotions are one regular form of activity. Sales may be promoted through the issuance of coupons to customers. This is a very exciting opportunity that customers do not fail to grab. The television, radio, and newspapers are avenues for advertisements for most companies, and a large group of customers and prospects are drawn to the sales floor through these effective means. Retail posters and point-of-sale displays are at retail stores from time to time. Contest boxes are situated at strategic points in the company during corporate or retail events, and contestants are given valuable gifts, which also advertise the company's products. Contest games such as scratch off for percentage or dollar discounts are part of the excitements.

Online events have gradually become outstanding. There are display accessories for retail supplies. Seasonal and holiday clearance of merchandise and products have not only been regular features of retail, but of bulk purchase businesses.

Patriotic holidays have been great opportunities to appeal to customers for more patronage and to attempt to draw prospects near.

Prices of products get marked down and further marked down by percentages while the goods last. It is always interesting to watch customers come to check to see whether products they want to buy have been marked down to the lowest possible. Some look round, identify what they like to buy, and ask whether they will soon be on sale or they may ask when they will be on sale. So many people like to buy when there are huge discounts. There are a few people who shop when they need to regardless of whether there is a markdown of prices or not.

Whatever may be the preference of the customers, the sales associate should use the sales promotion period to satisfy their customers' needs by giving them good customer service. The tendency in the crowded shopping situation is to give substandard service to customers. Some associates may be so tensed up that they fail to thank the customer for coming to do business with their company. Or after serving a customer, a salesperson may fail to acknowledge the next customer and can just proceed to check him out of the store without a word. Some may not have a smile on them.

The salesperson should by all means seize the opportunity of the busy period of sale to promote their company's products and goods and to close the sale. This is a good opportunity to build comeback clientele, and the advantage should be taken.

Seasonal and holiday clearance and sales are usually very colorful. Many people use the opportunity of shopping for social outings. Some proceed to the movie theater after the shopping spree. Others take their children on sightseeing, and others just lay about for relaxation. It is usually a beautiful sight at Christmas with the Father Christmas and the New Year season, which bring different dimensions of excitements to shopping Easter season, although by nature of the reason for celebrating it has a sober mood, it could be exciting. So also are the other seasons and holidays.

A large volume of business is done at these periods, and the associate should look forward to it for the opportunity of meeting customers' needs.

There are excitements for industry-related businesses even when they are going out of business. Companies that are going out of business need to sell all of their products and furniture and all capital investment features. The associates who work in these companies need to see even in this an opportunity to give good customer service. It is perhaps more needful that associates give good customer service since the company is closing finally and there is time restraint in getting the goods sold.

For companies that are opening new branches, there are advertisements posted on television, on newspapers, in posters, and on banners in multiple sizes. Opening a new business is an activity for a crowd. There are opening brochures and little token gifts given out to the invited guests, prospects, and customers. Sometimes there is good music provided. All these are in place for the benefit of the people. Then salespersons are to enjoy the beauty in the atmosphere and provide good customer service. Word of testimony from those who attend could bring very heavy referral to the company and put it in good standing.

Some companies and stores have added sale of catalogs to the responsibilities of their salespeople. The company catalogs satisfy the needs of customers who may not find the goods of their choice in the company or in the store. Sometimes when a company discontinues store sale of certain products, the catalogs do carry such products. The associate should have this information to give to customers who may be looking for items that are not in their stores.

When a customer is looking for a particular size or color or style of clothing, the associate should be able to suggest that the customer look in the catalog, and he is to lead him into searching from the book.

The associate should also offer to sell the catalog to the customer so that at his convenience, he can look for other goods he may still want. Some customers may prefer to do their own order at their homes; the associate should be willing to offer to do the order for them.

Company credit card application is becoming increasingly popular with stores and companies. The associate needs to understand how to talk to the customer so that he will understand the advantages of holding the credit card and will be willing to apply for one. One of the advantages of the credit card to the customer is that he is afforded the opportunity to buy what he needs even though he may not have the money to do so immediately. Another benefit is that the customer is able to buy at a good discount even if the items are already on sale. There is an immediate discount applicable on the day the credit line is approved, and there is an additional discount at the first time the card is to be used. The customer automatically becomes a mailing list member. The people get to see information of coming sales and clearances and could preview sales before others.

Once in a while, when the company does sale promotions, the cardholders get some additional percentage off their sale prices. The cardholders may get birthday and occasional gift certificates that entitle them to special sales and percentage or dollar discounts.

As long as the customer honors the contract conditions, he continues to enjoy the special deals.

On the side of the company, the use of their credit card by the company is an added gain. Whereas the company may not be losing when their customer pays for their goods with another company's card, check, or cash, the use of their credit cards help keep the money in the house with some added gains.

The use of the company's credit card is a way of controlling shrinkage. It is easier for the company to identify credit card fraud with their cards than with others. If the card is being used fraudulently, this is easier to detect if the customer is using the company's card than if he is using another company's.

The associate should appreciate that the sale of credit cards is to their advantage as workers. In the first place, the more money the company makes, the better their chances of salary increase and fulfillment of benefits. In the second instance, associates are usually paid some tokens for every credit card application that scales through screening. A little here and there is better than nothing, and the associate should see the need to be part of the company's programs.

Salespeople should try to suggest putting every sale on the company's credit cards if they have already. If they do not have, one is to suggest opening one to them so they can enjoy the discount. It's easy, and any sales associate can help the customer. The customer who gets one opened for him enjoys a discount on all purchases throughout the day on the first day and throughout the day on the day he uses the issued card for the first time.

Aggressive marketing techniques are used as companies grow by acquisition, services, and products. The salesperson lives through a lot of changes, and one day is usually not like the other. These varieties of activities and scenes revitalize the sales environment.

The salesperson should be aware of these excitements, look forward to them, enjoy them, and use them as opportunities to practice good customer service.

Retail Is A World of Incentives

It is possible that a new associate will be scared by the list of requirements that will be disseminated to him at the time of hire. It is also likely that he may become so intimidated that he may not want to continue with the job. But I have good news for any salesperson who feels that way. It is true that salesmanship is not an easy job, although a lot needs to be done to prevent this kind of feeling, but it is also true that good jobs done are rewarded. The criteria for reward and the quality of reward may need to be improved, but there is some reward for any associate who is worthy of compensation.

The world of retail is a world of "door busters" and "alternative pricing" of "buy one, get one free, or buy two or three and get one free." It could be a generous world of "buy one, pay 50 percent on the other, or buy one, pay $1 or 80k for the other."

Coupon scratching is another form of incentive, and this could be exciting to the customer as well as the associate as it is a kind of game.

The incentives stimulate the customers' interest in the company's products and goods, and they buy emotionally but usefully as well.

Sales representatives are not left out of these incentives. Most companies have the associate discount package come with their employment benefits. The percentage discount on purchases varies from company to company depending on the nature of business and the profit made. The discount applies to any purchase the associate makes as long as he is an employee of the company.

The salespeople become useful agents of company's products, and they promote their sales. It also provides the sales associates the opportunity to use their skills to boost sales. There is need for demonstration of stress-management tactics. The associate must be aware that they are cast members and that they have a vital role to play in the company's performance to the public. Even though sales associates are to smile in the performance of their duties, they had better be professional "smilers" at these special sales occasions in order to be good promoters of their company's products and even their own morale.

Conclusion

I wish to conclude my message in this book with an appeal. My appeal goes to the companies that are employers of retail labor as well as to the retail associates or salespeople.

I admonish every salesperson to do some search into their capabilities. I recommend that they arm themselves with necessary and useful information on the skill requirements of selling. I appeal to them to read this small book and give themselves an overview of the selling world to which they are about to enter. I like to believe that they will be willing to accept that they could be well fitted to that life, and they can decide to make a difference.

And should they, for any reason, not find the place where they work a suitable place for them and think they cannot adapt to the situation, the honorable thing to do is to bow out. It does not do the organization good or the salesperson any good if the salesperson pretentiously continues to work waiting for the least opportunity of another job offer to get out of the company. Unfortunately, economic situation may compel people to do this. But the sales floor is not the place for a pretender. The salesperson's attitude has so much impact on the company's fortune that no organization can afford to keep undedicated staff for any length of time.

I am eager for the employers of retail labor to be sensitive to the welfare of their salespeople. The customers are the key factor in retail, but the salespersons are important to the business as well as salesmen. Some companies would rather do without a salesperson than without a customer. At the instance of a customer reporting a salesperson for any reason to the company, some employers may take a hard-line attitude with the salesperson first before they ask the latter his own side of the story and even after the information.

The remuneration of salespeople needs an upward review. I believe when the attitude to sales and salespeople becomes more positive, the salary and benefits will change with that. The recruiting process, training, and retraining programs will witness a good revival along with any necessary changes. Of course, the whole picture of retail as a business will have a good new look.

My ambition in writing this book is to help employers of retail labor to enrich, improve, and increase their sales by making copies of this book available to their staff. I must say that I am more optimistic at this stage than when I wrote the earlier part of the book that employers of labor would make the book available for reading. What gave me this assurance was a new development that I saw recently. I saw a book column in the break room of a department store in a big shopping mall. The bookstand is standing at the corner of the room, and the caption on top of the shelf is written as "Book Share. Together, Sharing, Reading, Inspire." I checked out every book title, and all are mainly fiction books. There is no single book on business or on how the associates could improve his person on the job. I have not seen anything like this in any other store I had visited. This is not to say I am sure there is not one. For this store, this is a step in the right direction; and for others that do not have anything like this one, there is hope as well. It is a book that every training supervisor and every salesperson must read before and, continuously, after being hired. This book would assist the salespersons in building confidence for their job. The book, I believe, will bring into the sales profession potentially suitable people who may not have known that they could do well in retail sales business.

This is a book that every employer of retail and labor generally must read because it would furnish them with information that may help their businesses.

It is a book that I believe would do a lot of good to customers and prospects as it helps them to make right decisions in their purchases. By reading the book, the customers and prospects could help to make good salesmanship out of the salespeople as they become more understanding and cooperative.

Finally, this is a book that I believe will revolutionize the retail business in any part of the world in a very special way!

References

Andrews, Markita. 1986. *How to Sell More Cookies, Condos, Cadillacs, Computers, Computers . . . and Everything Else.* New York: Vintage Books A Division of Random House.

Brooks, William, T. 1992. *Niche Selling: How to Find Your Customer in a Crowded Market. IL: Business One*

Dapice, Rocco, (Article) 2005.There's a Mouse in the Classroom. Indiana: *Christian Womanhood*, First Baptist Church of Hammond

Girard, Joe. 1995. *Mastering Your Way to the Top.* NY: Warner Books, Inc.

Jolles, Robert. 1995. *Customer Centered Selling.* New York: Free Press.

Kimball, Bob. 1994. *Successful Selling. IL: NTC Business Books, a division of NTC Publishing Group.*

Leboeuf, Michael. 1996. The Perfect Business-How to Make a Million from Home. New York: Simon & Schuster.

Mitchell, Garry. 1991. *The Heart of the Sale: Making the Customers Need to Buy-the Key to Successful Selling. New York: AMACOM, a division of American Management Association.*

Penney, J.C.1994.*Human Resource Department: Tips for Sales Professionals.*

Rogak, Lisa. 1999. *Smart Guide to Starting a Small Business. New York: John Wiley & Sons*

www.ingramcontent.com/pod-product-compliance
Lightning Source LLC
Chambersburg PA
CBHW022134170526
45157CB00004B/1873